# HOW TO USE THE POWER IN THE BLOOD OF JESUS FOR A RESULT-ORIENTED PRAYER

**Prophet Johnson Akinfenwa**

## How to Use The Power In The Blood Of Jesus For a Result-Oriented Prayer:

ISBN-13: 978-1999711405

Unless otherwise indicated, all Scripture quotations are taken from the King James Version (KJV). All rights reserved.

# *DEDICATION*

This book is dedicated to God the Father, the Son and the Holy Spirit who has anointed and bestowed the enabling grace over my life to write this book.

Therefore, I wholeheartedly dedicate this book to the glory and honour of the everlasting kingdom of God.

MARANATHA!!!!

# CONTENTS

# *ACKNOWLEDGEMENT*

First and foremost, I want to acknowledge the Almighty God, the giver of my life. I give Him praise, honour, glory and adoration. I also give thanks to Jesus who enabled me to write and draw out the content of this book from the prophetic well of living water which He put inside of me. Praise and thanks to the Holy Spirit my great Teacher and the source of my inspiration who endowed me with fresh revelation to write this book.

At this point, I will like to express my uncanny appreciation to my dear friend and co-worker in the Service of the Kingdom, Apostle Ola Thomas Ojo. He is the Presiding Apostle over Christ Temple International based in the United Kingdom. I owe him my appreciation for taking his time to meticulously read through the manuscript of this book, making sure that the focus of this book is in line with the scripture and void of heresy. In addition to reading through, he also took his time to write the foreword for the book as an expression of his endorsement that the book will bless the body of Christ globally. Thank you so much, and I pray that God will honour and increase his anointing upon you, with good health and long life.

Also, my immense thanks to my wonderful daughter Charissa Ibiyemi Akinfenwa for her support by sacrificing some of her precious time in typing the manuscript in preparation for publication. Thank you and God bless you daughter.

Finally, my heartfelt thanks to my beloved wife, Pastor Funmilola Akinfenwa for her encouragement, support, suggestions and her patience which helps me a lot to concentrate on writing this book. In the same way, I will like to appreciate my sons- Emmanuel and Israel Akinfenwa whose words of encouragement and support served as a source of inspiration to complete this book writing project. I also appreciate my wonderful daughters Daniella, Grace and Tobi (my daughter-in-law) for their unceasing prayers for me. I give praise to God for such a wonderful family that God has blessed me with especially my wife and our lovely children who believed in the calling of God upon my life.

# *FOREWORD*

I count it a great honour and privilege to write the foreword to this book titled, HOW TO USE THE POWER IN THE BLOOD OF JESUS FOR A RESULT-ORIENTED PRAYER by Prophet Johnson Akinfenwa.

I have known the author since 1996 as a lovely, faithful and humble man of God with a prophetic mantle who proclaims the Word of God with grace, clarity and precision.

His simplicity and gracious use of words which everyone can easily and perfectly understand, in the preaching and teaching of the Gospel are often accompanied with divine power, signs and wonders.

The truth of the book is simple, clear and concise: The blood of the LORD Jesus Christ still works as it will never lose its power.

While reading and meditating the content of each chapter of this book, you will rediscover the Voice in the Blood which absolutely no one can silence. This holy Voice will also guide and guard your prayer life.

You will find the amazing way of turning the battle against your enemies by the right application of the absolute, unlimited and unstoppable power in the blood of Jesus.
There are divine security and protection in the blood which you can activate in every area of your life.

You can also use the secret power of this most holy Blood for the effective reconciliation and efficient restoration of all broken relationships to the glory of God our Eternal Father.

Another excellent and exciting revelation is discovering how to secure the Presence, glory and blessing of God by activating the power in the blood of Jesus ultimately leading to your exponential spiritual growth and uncommon financial abundance.

Having thoroughly read and examined the content and context thereof, it's my pleasure and delight to recommend this book to all and especially those seeking after the truth and power in the holy blood of the Lamb of God, our LORD and Saviour Jesus Christ.

As I have been profoundly blessed and inspired, I do not have any hesitation whatsoever in recommending this book to you. You will be exhorted, edified and comforted.

Go ahead and be blessed too.

Apostle Ola Thomas Ojo

Christ Temple International London
Author of Activating the Power of God within
You: The Anointing

# CHAPTER ONE:
## INTRODUCTION

The burden to write this book was imposed upon my spirit by the Holy Spirit. It explains how to use the power in the blood of Jesus as a weapon of warfare to secure victory when confronted with difficult battles of life.

Therefore, the book is written to enable believers to have an understanding on how to invoke the power in the blood of Jesus as an effective force to engage in spiritual battles. This strategy had been foreshadowed in the Old Testament whenever God made prescription for sacrificing animal blood in different occasions. We are to exercise the power in the blood of Jesus by faith through prayer to launch offensive attacks against the camp of the adversary to take back all that he (Satan) has stolen from our territories...business, marriage, family, ministry, health, etc. Even the angels in heaven when engaged in battle with Satan invoked the prevailing power in the blood of Jesus to secure victory over Satan and all his cohorts... Halleluyah!

*"And they overcame him by the blood of the Lamb, and
by the word of their testimony; and they loved not their
lives unto the death."(Revelation 12:11)*

Another profound revelation is about what the
Bible says, that the blood speaks and God
Himself speaks through the blood. The most
revealing scripture to buttress this fact is
Numbers 7:88-89:

*"And all the oxen for the sacrifice of the peace offerings
were twenty and four bullocks, the rams sixty, the he
goats sixty, the lambs of the first year sixty. This was
the dedication of the altar, after that it was anointed.
And when Moses was gone into the tabernacle of the
congregation to speak with him, then he heard the
voice of one speaking unto him from off the mercy seat
that was upon the ark of testimony, from between the
two cherubims: and he spake unto him."*

From the above content, we see that blood
sacrifice was offered as required by God. Some of
this blood was spread on the mercy seat which
covered the Ark, overlooking by two Golden
Angels. The Ark was stationed and preserved in
the Tent of meeting. The most interesting part of
the scenario was that as Moses entered into the
tent of meeting to speak with the LORD, 'he
heard the voice speaking to him from the above
the mercy seat that was upon the Ark of
Testimony from the between the two Cherubims:
And He spoke to Moses.' WOW! The voice of

12

God came through the blood that was on the mercy seat. This means the voice of God came to Moses through the blood...the blood speaks!

This is what God revealed to Apostle Paul in Hebrews 12:24. God speaks to the church today, no more through the blood of animals which was the shadow of the blood of Jesus, the Lamb of God that took away the sins of the whole world. But God speaks now to believers through the blood of Jesus.

*Hebrews 12:24 (AMP)*
*"And to Jesus, the Mediator of a new covenant [uniting God and man], and to the sprinkled blood, which speaks [of mercy], a better and nobler and more gracious message than the blood of Abel [which cried out for vengeance]."*

God has made the blood of Jesus available to us as our weapon of warfare. What we need to do is to dip our faith in the prevailing power of the blood. God speaks mercy, victory, blessings, breakthrough, success, redemption, justification, cleansing, peace and so on to the Body of Christ through the blood of Jesus today.

Obviously, God has made the holy blood of the LORD Jesus Christ available to us as our weapon of warfare. What we really need to do is to maintain our deepest faith in the prevailing power of the blood to make our prayer effective and result-oriented. Hallelujah!

However, I will like to suggest here that you need to examine yourself before you begin to pray with the blood of Jesus. And if you discover any sin or shortcoming in your life, repent and ask for forgiveness before you begin to use the power in the blood of Jesus for your prayer. Psalm 66:18-19(NLT) says:

*"If I had not confessed the sin in my heart, the Lord would not have listened. But God did listen! He paid attention to my prayer."*

I pray that the blood of Jesus will speak better things to your life as you pray by the power in the blood. Amen!

## CHAPTER TWO:
## FOURTEEN FUNDAMENTAL UNIQUENESS ABOUT THE BLOOD OF JESUS AND ITS IMPORTANCE IN OUR PRAYER TO GOD.

It is important for me to pass this fundamental truth about the reason why the blood of Jesus is unique. The Holy Spirit revealed this to me in one of the moments of my prayer and meditation in the presence of the Lord. It is for this reason that I am encouraging every believer to put their absolute faith in the immeasurable power of the HOLY BLOOD OF JESUS. Believers must bear all these fundamental truths in mind at all times:

1. There is a voice in the blood of Jesus which no one(including Satan and all his demons) can silence. (Hebrews 12:24)

2. There is power in the blood of Jesus which cannot be confronted or defeated by Satan, principalities, powers, the rulers of the darkness of this world and the spiritual wickedness in high places. (Revelation 12:7-11)

3) There is abundant life eternal in the blood of Jesus which cannot be destroyed by any means. (Hebrews 9:12; John 10: 10-18)

4) Both the Holy Spirit and the Word are accountable to the witness of the blood of Jesus. (1John 5:8-9, Leviticus 9:6-9,18-24, John 1: 29, 34-36)

5) There is no situation in a believer's life, no matter how difficult which the power in the blood cannot reconcile or resolve. (Ephesians 2:13-16; Colossians 1: 20-22)

6) It was through the power (virtue) in the blood of Jesus that God raised up Jesus from the dead. (Hebrews 13:20)

7) God Almighty's power was not exerted to raise up Jesus from the dead, apart from the power in the blood of Jesus. (Ephesians 1:19-20 AMP)

8) It was through the shedding of His Holy blood that He released the eternal life hidden in the same blood and making it(eternal life) available to us when He rose up from the death through

resurrection.(Hebrews 10:10-14; Isaiah 53:12)

9) The efficacy of His blood satisfied the law and righteousness of God and this made the righteousness of God to be imputed on believers immediately we confess Jesus Christ as our Lord and Saviour.(Hebrews 10:14; Hebrews 9:30; Romans 3:21-22; 2Corinthians 5:21; Romans 10:4)

10) The life in His blood was exchanged for death when He shed His blood on the Cross of Calvary, hence death, sin and corruption were defeated when He rose up from the death through the power of resurrection.(Matthew27:45-55; Romains 8:1-11)

11) There is power in the blood of Jesus which has the efficacy to permanently delete every hand writing of Satan against your life. (Colossians 2:13-16)

12) The Almightiness of the power of God is exclusively embedded inside the blood of Jesus. This is the main reason why Apostle Paul prayed for the Ephesians church that they might have full

revelation of this fundamental truth.(Ephesians 1:16-23)

13) Through the power in the blood of Jesus, believers have been purified, set apart/consecrated as holy unto God.(Hebrews 13:12;1Peters 2:9-10)

14) The power in the blood of Jesus opens the life gate which God had shut against Adam and Eve according to Genesis 3:22-24. But when Jesus shed His blood on the Cross the life gate was opened (Paradise) and gave us access to God's presence.(Zechariah 13:1-2; John 19: 34; Mathew 27:50-51; Hebrews 4:14-16; Ephesians 2:6,13; Hebrews 10:16-23)

Many might want to find out how the blood speaks. The answer to this is revealed in the two scriptural quotations below:

*"And there are three that bear witness in earth, the Spirit, and the water, and the blood: and these three agree in one." 1 (John 5:8)*

*"And to Jesus the mediator of the new covenant, and to the blood of sprinkling, that speaketh better things than that of Abel." (Hebrews 12:24)*

From the texts above we notice that the blood is one of the three that bear witness on the earth and is the one that speaks for believers in heaven. Since the function of a witness especially in the Court of Law is to speak and give account of what he saw in an incident, then based on this fact, the blood of Jesus being a witness must have voice and capacity to speak `better things on behalf of believers.

**Therefore, by the witness of the blood of Jesus, I declare and I decree that the blood of Jesus will speak victory, blessings, manifold wisdom, uncommon favour and progress over your life in Jesus name.**

In each of the chapters of this book, there is a short exhortation with relevant scriptures. This is to give understanding to the readers on how to apply relevant scriptures using the blood of Jesus as our spiritual weapons for effective prayer and intercession.

As God releases upon us the spirit of grace and supplication, it is my prayer that the blood will speak for you and make your prayer to be effective and result–oriented in Jesus name.

*Zechariah 12:10 (NKJV):*
*"I will pour out on the house of David and on the people of Jerusalem, the Spirit of grace (unmerited favour) and supplication. And they will look at Me whom they have pierced;..."*

# LET    THE    BLOOD    SPEAK!

## CHAPTER THREE:
## VICTORY OVER THE ADVERSARY BY THE POWER INTHE BLOOD

In this chapter, we are going to see how the children of Israel prevailed over their enemies(the Philistines) by the combination of the intercessory prayer of Prophet Samuel and their faith in the prevailing power of the blood of the lamb(prophetic lamb).

This principle confirms Revelation 12:11 (AMPC)

*And they have overcome (conquered) him by means of the blood of the Lamb and by the utterance of their testimony, for they did not love and cling to life even when faced with death [holding their lives cheap till they had to die for their witnessing.*

Therefore, the prayer strategies used in the chapter below is prophetic intercession and the power in the blood as our weapon of victory over the enemies of our progress. In this scenario, the Philistines were the enemies of the children of Israel.

*"Now when the Philistines heard that the Israelites had gathered at Mizpah, the lords of the Philistines went up against Israel. And when the Israelites heard of it, they were afraid of the Philistines And the Israelites said to*

21

*Samuel, Do not cease to cry to the Lord our God for us that He may save us from the hand of the Philistines. So Samuel took a sucking lamb and offered it as a whole burnt offering to the Lord; and Samuel cried to the Lord for Israel, and the Lord answered him. As Samuel was offering up the burnt offering, the Philistines drew near to attack Israel. But the Lord thundered with a great voice that day against the Philistines and threw them into confusion, and they were defeated before Israel. And the men of Israel went out of Mizpah and pursued the Philistines and smote them as far as below Beth-car. Then Samuel took a stone and set it between Mizpah and Shen, and he called the name of it Ebenezer [stone of help], saying, Heretofore the Lord has helped us."*
*(1 Samuel 7:7-12 AMPC)*

At this point, believers are encouraged to learn to invoke the power in the blood of Jesus combined with intercessory prayer in order to prevail over the enemies and their manifestations in various form and to secure the restoration of lost blessings, opportunities and lost territories.

### PRAYER POINTS:

1. **Father in the name of Jesus and by the power in the blood of Jesus the LAMB of God, I decree that every power and conspiracy of the enemies of my soul be destroyed by the power in the blood of Jesus. Let thunder and God's anger**

22

from heaven fall upon my adversaries,
throwing them into confusion and
render them powerless until they are
subdued in Jesus name.

2. By the power in the blood of Jesus, I
demand for full restoration of all the
blessings and inheritance stolen from
my life, stolen from my family, stolen
from my business in the name of Jesus.
(1Samuel 7:14)

3. By the power in the blood of Jesus, I
demand for a 'token' and a sign of
victory as a testimony (stone of help)
and evidence that God has answered
my prayer in Jesus. Amen! (1Samuel
7:12)

*"For a great door and effectual is opened unto me, and
there are many adversaries."(1Corinthians16:9)*

4. Father, by the power in the holy blood
of Jesus, I decree and I legislate against
the adversaries working to upset my
breakthrough, my success and my
progress in the mighty name of Jesus.
Also, I pray in Jesus name that doors of
opportunity shut against me be opened
speedily by their own accord. By the
blood of Jesus, I call for angelic
assistance to go ahead of me to
different nations, to break into pieces
the gates of brass and cut asunder the

bars of iron, releasing into my hands the treasure of darkness and the hidden riches of secret places in Jesus name. (Isaiah 45:2-3)

5. LORD God Almighty, by the power in the blood of Jesus I confess, decree and prophecy Joel 2:21-27 for the restoration of the lost years, lost opportunities, blessings and lost territories:

*"Fear not, O land; be glad and rejoice: for the LORD will do great things. Be not afraid, ye beasts of the field: for the pastures of the wilderness do spring, for the tree beareth her fruit, the fig tree and the vine do yield their strength. Be glad then, ye children of Zion, and rejoice in the LORD your God: for he hath given you the former rain moderately, and he will cause to come down for you the rain, the former rain, and the latter rain in the first month. And the floors shall be full of wheat, and the vats shall overflow with wine and oil. And I will restore to you the years that the locust hath eaten, the cankerworm, and the caterpillar, and the palmerworm, my great army which I sent among you. And ye shall eat in plenty, and be satisfied, and praise the name of the LORD your God that hath dealt wondrously with you: and my people shall never be ashamed. And ye shall know that I am in the midst of Israel, and that I am the LORD your God, and none else: and my people shall never be ashamed." Amen!*

# CHAPTER FOUR:
## TURNING THE BATTLE AGAINST YOUR ENEMIES BY THE POWER IN THE BLOOD OF JESUS

*"And when the king of Moab saw that the battle was too sore for him, he took with him seven hundred men that drew swords, to break through even unto the king of Edom: but they could not. Then he took his eldest son that should have reigned in his stead, and offered him for a burnt offering upon the wall. And there was great indignation against Israel: and they departed from him, and returned to their own land."*
*(2King 3:26-27)*

At this point, for the purpose of clarification, I will like to say that it is the revelatory application of the above scripture that I want to highlight in this passage to draw a parallel on how believers can make use of the Holy Blood of Jesus to turn the battle against the enemies in spiritual warfare. The scripture above is very significant because it will teach us how to make use of the power in the Holy Blood of Jesus as New Testament believers to secure breakthrough and turning the battles against our enemies. Though, the human blood that was shed in the above scripture was not according to the will of God. However, in parallel, I will like to use its application to drive home my point on how to make use of the power in the blood of Jesus the only begotten Son of the Almighty God. Satan

25

understands the power in the blood of human beings right from the time when Cain killed Abel. That is why people in the secret occult in the dark world, herbalists, witches/witchdoctors, etc, like to demand for animal or human blood for their evil acts and rituals to appease Satan in the dark world in order to make their evil intention effective by invoking the power of the blood. In the above scripture, the children of Israel were supposed to know better, the power in sacrificing the blood of prophetic animals at the altar while the battle was going on. But they failed to keep the sacrificial altar alive with prescribed blood of prophetic lambs.

But in order to corrupt what the Holy Blood of Jesus will do for believers in the New Testament, I believe Satan suggested to the king of Moab to sacrifice his only son that will reign after him (this idea cannot be from God). Therefore, the revelation I am bringing to us as people of God is the application of the HOLY BLOOD of Jesus as a weapon of WARFARE to turn the wrath and indignation of God against our enemies where and when we are facing with intense battles and challenges of life. The most thrilling part of the scripture above is the phrase,

*"And when the king of Moab saw that the battles was too sore for him...Then he took his eldest son that*

*should have reigned in his stead, and offered him for a
burnt offering upon the wall. And there was great
indignation against Israel: and they departed from
him, and returned to their own land."*

We see in the passage that the king put his trust
first in the ability of men to help him out to
secure breakthrough (700 elite armies). But the
ability and the expertise of men failed. It was
after this that the king therefore resulted in
shedding the blood of his son who was supposed
to reign after him. This was a corrupt way of
foreshadowing what the Holy Blood of Jesus will
do for believers eventually. This act of sacrificing
the blood of his son secured the expected
breakthrough and won the battle for him without
shooting any arrow or gun. The power of the
human blood provoked satanic indignation
which turned the battle against Israel (the people
of God), and giving victory to the King of Moab.
Therefore, the point I am try to get across is this,
if the power in the shed blood of an ordinary
man brought breakthrough and turned the battle
against the armies of the children of Israel, how
much more will the power in the Holy Blood of
Jesus turn the battle against the enemies of the
children of God? THERE IS A
BREAKTHROUGH POWER IN THE BLOOD OF
JESUS... HALLELUYAH!!!

When Jesus died and shed His blood on the cross, the power in His blood became our ALMIGHTYFORCE and our SUPERNATURAL WEAPON OF VICTORY IN WARFARE. Praise God!

*"For the weapons of our warfare are not carnal, but mighty through God to the pulling down of strong holds..." (2Corinthians 10:4)*

### PRAYER POINTS:

1) In the name of Jesus, I put upon myself the invincible armour of warfare which is in the blood of Jesus. I confess and I declare that the weapons of my warfare are not carnal, but mighty through the power in the blood of Jesus and my victory is always guaranteed.

2) By the power in the blood of Jesus I secure my breakthrough in every area of my life in Jesus name.

3) In the name of Jesus, and by the power in the blood of Jesus, I decree God's anger and indignation against the enemies of my peace.

4) By the prevailing power in the blood of Jesus, I turn the battle against the

enemies of my progress, my success, my marriage, my promotion, my business in Jesus name.

5) In Jesus name and by the power in His blood, let the terror of God trouble the heart of my enemies until they turn back. Let them fall and never to rise again in Jesus name. Amen! (2 King 3:27).

6) In the name of Jesus and by the power in the blood of Jesus let my enemies suffer defeat, disgrace and cloth them with the garment of shame in Jesus name. Amen!

7) In Jesus name and by the power in the blood, I petition the heavens to turn the battle against all my adversaries, and I command them to turn back and back out of my life and out of my territories in Jesus name.

## CHAPTER FIVE:
## LET THE BLOOD OF JESUS PURSUE MY ENEMIES

*Therefore, as I live, saith the Lord GOD, I will prepare thee unto blood, and blood shall pursue thee: seeth thou hast not hated blood, even blood shall pursue thee.(Ezekiel 35:6)*

In the scripture above, we can see how powerful the blood is. It has supernatural dynamics and capacity to pursue your enemies both in the physical and spiritual realm. These are the enemies who are determined to see your end at the time of your weakness and vulnerability. The prevailing power of the HOLY BLOOD of Jesus is available to pursue your enemies, fighting your battle and secure your victory in Jesus name.

### PRAYER POINTS:

1) **Father, in the name of Jesus, I decree and I declare that the power in the blood of Jesus will pursue my enemies until they perish in the same way that Pharaoh and all his armies perished in the Red sea. Amen!**

2) **By the power in the blood of Jesus, I seek for the assistance of warrior angels to pursue my adversaries and a total stop to their plans and diabolical intensions planned against me, my**

31

**family, my business, my marriage, my
progress, my finances, my health, my
ministry in Jesus name.**

3) **I decree and I declare by the prevailing
power in the blood of Jesus that angels
of God pursue and put a stop to every
satanic activity, demonic movement
and decoy set up by Satan through
human agents to cause my downfall.**

4) **Father, in the name of Jesus, I decree
and I declare that you turn the battle
against all my enemies in the same way
you turned the battle against Pharaoh
and the Egyptians by the power in the
blood of the Lamb.**

5) **Let the power in the blood of Jesus
pursue all my enemies until they
surrender in Jesus name. Amen!**

# CHAPTER SIX:
## DIVINE SECURITY AND PROTECTION BY THE POWER IN THE BLOOD.

*"Speak ye unto all the congregation of Israel, saying, In the tenth day of this month they shall take to them every man a lamb, according to the house of their fathers, a lamb for a house: And if the household be too little for the lamb, let him and his neighbour next unto his house take it according to the number of the souls; every man according to his eating shall make your count for the lamb. For I will pass through the land of Egypt this night, and will smite all the firstborn in the land of Egypt, both man and beast; and against all the gods of Egypt I will execute judgment: I am the LORD. And the blood shall be to you for a token upon the houses where ye are: and when I see the blood, I will pass over you, and the plague shall not be upon you to destroy you, when I smite the land of Egypt. Then Moses called for all the elders of Israel, and said unto them, Draw out and take you a lamb according to your families, and kill the Passover. And ye shall take a bunch of hyssop, and dip it in the blood that is in the bason, and strike the lintel and the two side posts with the blood that is in the bason; and none of you shall go out at the door of his house until the morning. For the LORD will pass through to smite the Egyptians; and when he seeth the blood upon the lintel, and on the two side posts, the LORD will pass over the door, and will not suffer the destroyer to come in unto your houses to smite you.(Exodus 12:3-13, 21-24).*

The above passage is very vital to the understanding of the power in the blood in ensuring and assuring God's divine security and protection against the <u>destroyer</u> (Satan). What we see in the content of the passage is the fact that the blood has supreme power to overcome the destroyer.

In verse 23, God said he would not permit the "destroyer" to enter into their homes to visit them with death. At this point, it will be worth noting to identify who the destroyer is according to Revelation 9:11.

*"And they had a king over them which is the angel of the bottomless pit, whose name in the Hebrew tongue is Abaddon but in the Greek tongue has his name "Apollyon"*

In the above scripture, both 'Abaddon' in Hebrew and 'Apollyon' in Greek mean "destroyer." So the great destroyer is none other than Satan, the king of the demons of the bottomless pit.

Praise be to God that by the power in the blood of Jesus, we have been saved from the kingdom of darkness (kingdom of the destroyer).

*"Giving thanks unto the Father, which hath made us meet to be partakers of the inheritance of the saints in light: Who hath delivered us from the power of darkness, and hath translated us into the kingdom of*

*his dear Son: In whom we have redemption through his blood, even the forgiveness of sins:(Colossians 1:12-14).*

## PRAYERS POINTS:

1) Father, I thank You for the power in the blood of Jesus, Your only begotten son who shed His blood on the cross to set me free from sin and the kingdom of darkness. I also thank You my dear heavenly Father that by the power in the blood of Your son Jesus, all my sins in the past have been erased and a new calendar and a new chapter of life is opened for me.

2) In the name of Jesus, I am protected by the prevailing power in the blood of Jesus.

3) In the name of Jesus, I disallow the intrusion and the entry of the destroyer (Satan) into my house, my marriage, my business, my ministry and my children. I am divinely protected by the blood of Jesus.

4) My heavenly Father, I plead the blood of Jesus over my life, family, business, career, health and my destiny as a token of divine security against the attack and the arrows of the enemy. It

is written, no weapon formed against me shall prosper by the power in the blood of Jesus. By the power in the blood of Jesus, I reverse the effect of every negative spoken word against me and my destiny in Jesus name. Amen

5) In the name of Jesus, I decree and I confess that every satanic handwriting of the wicked is completely erased and blotted out by the power in the blood of Jesus. I confess Your words according to Colossians 2:13-15 AMP:

*"When you were dead in your sins and in the uncircumcision of your flesh (worldliness, manner of life), God made you alive together with Christ, having [freely] forgiven us all our sins, having cancelled out the certificate of debt consisting of legal demands [which were in force] against us and which were hostile to us. And this certificate He has set aside and completely removed by nailing it to the cross. When He had disarmed the rulers and authorities [those supernatural forces of evil operating against us], He made a public example of them [exhibiting them as captives in His triumphal procession], having triumphed over them through the cross."*

6) In the name of Jesus, I pray according to Your word in Isaiah 49:25. The Lord of host contends with those who contend with me, and they shall be drunk with their own blood. By the blood of Jesus, I demand for full

restoration of all that had been stolen away from me and my family. I receive them back as compensation in sevenfold in Jesus name. Amen! As you compensated the children of Israel with the Egyptian spoils, I demand for the same by the blood of Jesus.

*Exodus 12:36:*
*"The LORD gave the people favor in the sight of the Egyptians, so that they gave them what they asked. And so they plundered the Egyptians [of those things]."*

7) In the name of Jesus, I decree and I confess that as God delivered and protected the children of Israel from the destroyer by the power in the blood, so also I decree that I am delivered from every bondage of the enemy in whatever manifestations in Jesus name. I am shielded and protected from satanic arrows of sickness, poverty, failure, disappointment, misfortunes, mental break down and pre-mature death. In Jesus name I sprinkle the blood of Jesus on every aspect of my life in Jesus name. Amen!

8) Father, in the name of Jesus as the blood secured protection and salvation of every member of the family of the

children of Israel, I declare and I petition the heaven that by the blood of Jesus every member of my family (husband, wife, children) is saved by the invincible power of the blood of Jesus. Amen!

## CHAPTER SEVEN:
## JOB AND HIS HOUSEHOLD WERE PROTECTED BY THE POWER IN THE BLOOD.

*Then Satan answered the LORD, and said, Doth Job fear God for nought? Hast not thou made an hedge about him, and about his house, and about all that he hath on every side? thou hast blessed the work of his hands, and his substance is increased in the land. But put forth thine hand now, and touch all that he hath, and he will curse thee to thy face. And the LORD said unto Satan, Behold, all that he hath is in thy power; only upon himself put not forth thine hand. So Satan went forth from the presence of the LORD.(Job1:9-12)*

According to the above scripture, (vs10) Job and his household were protected by God in five major areas and I will outline these five areas in paraphrase:

(i)     His personal life was protected, "...hast thou not made an hedge about him"(vs 10a)

(ii)    His entire household was protected "...an hedge about his house"(vs 10b)

(iii)   All his possessions/belongings are protected "...hedge about all that he hath on every side"(vs 10c)

(iv)   All his undertakings were blessed and protected "...hedge all around the work of his hand..."(vs 10d)

(v)    All his scope of influence prospered and protected (e.g. business, relationship, connection, social status) "...hedge around his substance in the land"(vs 10e)


It is important to note historically that Job always gave blood sacrifice to God daily as an act of his worship to God. For this reason, the power in the blood gave him divine protection in those five major areas which Satan put on the spotlight while accusing him (Job) before God.


## PRAYER POINTS

### HEDGE OF PROTECTION AROUND MY PERSONAL LIFE

1) **In the name of Jesus, I pray and confess that my personal life is protected by the blood of Jesus against sickness, diseases, misfortunes, premature death and failure. No weapon formed against me shall prosper and, every tongue that speaks against me, my wife or my children is condemned by the blood of Jesus. I**

enjoy divine insurance because I am marked by the blood of Jesus. Amen!

## HEDGE OF PROTECTION AROUND MY HOUSEHOLD

My Father, in the name of Jesus I pray that the power in the blood of Jesus will form a strategic canopy of protection around my entire household against the invasion of the enemies. By the power in the blood of Jesus there shall be no perforation or penetration of Satanic attack against my wife, my children and everything that concerns me in Jesus name.

I agree with your words according to Psalm 144:12:

*"That our sons may be as plants grown up in their youth; that our daughters may be as corner stones, polished after the similitude of a palace:"*

Your word says my sons shall be as plants grown up in their youth; and my daughters shall be as corner stones, polished after the similitude of palaces. Your word also established that great shall be the peace of my children. Therefore, by the power in the blood of Jesus, I secure all these promises for

41

**all my children and grandchildren in the name of Jesus. Amen!**

## HEDGE OF PROTECTION AROUND MY POSSESSIONSAND BELONGINGS

I agree with your words according to Psalm 144:13-15:

*"That our garners may be full, affording all manner of store: that our sheep may bring forth thousands and ten thousands in our streets: That our oxen may be strong to labour; that there be no breaking in, nor going out; that there be no complaining in our streets. Happy is that people, that is in such a case: yea, happy is that people, whose God is the LORD."*

**God of heavens and the earth, I decree and declare that divine security be put around every perimeter of my belongings and possessions by the blood of Jesus. In the name of Jesus, we are insured against calamities and misfortunes of any kind as I sprinkle the blood of Jesus over all my possessions for divine protection. Amen!**

## HEDGE OF PROTECTION AROUND MY UNDERTAKINGS

In the name of Jesus, I confess and I pray that all my undertakings are blessed and protected by the blood of Jesus. The word of the LORD says:

*"Blessed is the man that walketh not in the counsel of the ungodly, nor standeth in the way of sinners, nor sitteth in the seat of the scornful. But his delight is in the law of the LORD; and in his law doth he meditate day and night. And he shall be like a tree planted by the rivers of water, that bringeth forth his fruit in his season; his leaf also shall not wither; and whatsoever he doeth shall prosper."(Psalm 1:1-3)*

By the power in the blood of Jesus, I invoke the authority in the Word of God and His covenant promises that in the name of Jesus whatsoever I lay my hands upon, whatsoever my children and children's children lay their hands upon shall prosper and be protected by the blood of Jesus. Amen!

## HEDGE OF PROTECTION AROUND MY SCOPE OF INFLUENCE

My heavenly Father, in the name of Jesus I decree and declare that a strong wall of protection and defence be established around my scope of influences, physically, spiritually, business, ministry, relationship. By the power in the blood of Jesus, I prohibit and forbid the influence of Satanic agents, warlocks, character assassination, tale bearers, prognosticators, false accusers and vision killers. I invoke the authority of God's covenant promise for me, that no weapon formed against me shall prosper, and every tongue raised against me is condemned because I am protected by the blood of Jesus. Amen!

# CHAPTER EIGHT:
## RECONCILIATION AND RESTORATION OF BROKEN RELATIONSHIP BY THE POWER IN THE BLOOD OF JESUS

We are living at a time when Satan is doing everything to destroy different forms of relationship. Satan started this evil undertaking in the Garden of Eden when he destroyed the relationship between God and man. But praise be to God who in His mercy, made a special provision to facilitate reconciliation and restoration of relationship, starting with Himself and man. God made this possible when He offered the blood of His son on the cross of Calvary. As confirmed in Ephesians 2:13-16:

*"But now in Christ Jesus ye who sometimes were far off are made nigh by the blood of Christ. For he is our peace, who hath made both one, and hath broken down the middle wall of partition between us; Having abolished in his flesh the enmity, even the law of commandments contained in ordinances; for to make in himself of twain one new man, so making peace; And that he might reconcile both unto God in one body by the cross, having slain the enmity thereby:*

The above scripture is self-explanatory, and in this content I will outline what the power in the blood of Jesus did to achieve the reconciliation and restoration of our relationship with Himself and with ourselves, both Jews and Gentiles.

Therefore, when Jesus shed His blood on the cross:

- He united us first with Himself (vs13)

- The power in His blood brought us nearer to God after about 4,000 years of man being separated from God. (vs13)

- The blood of Jesus brought peace into the broken relationship. (vs 14)

- The blood of Jesus brought unity by removing separation between Jews and Gentiles making them to be one people (vs 14)

- The blood of Jesus destroyed the power of <u>separation</u> and <u>hostility</u> which put relationship apart either between God and man or in between human beings e.g. husband and wife. (vs 14)

- The blood of Jesus has the power to bring together different groups of people or fragmented dysfunctional members of the same family e.g. husband and wife, parents and children. The power in the blood is able to unite them to form one new people or one new family living together in peace (vs 15)

- Jesus was able to effect the reconciliation and restoration of all forms of broken relationship by the power inHis shed blood on the cross of Calvary. (vs 16)

- The power in the blood of Jesus has the capacity to destroy and put to death hostility between two individuals(or between parents and children)thereby facilitating forgiveness and peace (vs 16)

## PRAYER POINTS:

## RECONCILIATION AND RESTORATION OF BROKEN MARITAL RELATIONSHIP

**Father, in the name of Jesus by the power in the blood of Jesus, I come against hostility and separation between myself and my husband/wife. In Jesus name, I superimpose unity, peace and full reconciliation over my marital relationship, because the blood of Jesus had paid for it on the cross of Calvary. And according to Ephesians 2:13 the blood of Jesus has closed the gap of separation between us, and the same power in the blood has drawn us closer (as husband and wife) together as one family in Jesus name.**

Furthermore, I pray that the blood of Jesus speaks to our hearts and cleanse our conscience to repent and forgive one another in the same way as God forgives all our sins through the atoning blood of Jesus. I pray for the conviction of the Holy Spirit to humble us that we may allow the love of Christ in our hearts to take pre-eminence over our marital relationship in Jesus name. Amen! Therefore, I believe and by faith that as from this day onwards my marriage relationship is fully restored and reconciled by the Holy Blood of Jesus. Amen!

## RECONCILIATION AND RESTORATION OF A DYSFUNCTIONAL FAMILY.

Father, in the name of Jesus, I pray for the reconciliation and restoration between distant fathers/mothers and their children. In Jesus name and by the power of Holy Spirit I rebuke and I decree against the spirit responsible for broken homes and dysfunctional families. The Lord promised in His Word that through the power of the Holy Spirit, He will turn the heart of fathers to the children and the heart of the children to their fathers. I pray for a strong bond of love between the immediate members of my families (parent and children).

Therefore, by the power in the blood of Jesus I build a strong hedge and spiritual boundary around my family especially my children making it impenetrable to the attack of Satan and his demons. Furthermore, in the name of Jesus and by the power in the blood of Jesus, I put a stop to the operations of the demon spirit that breaks apart marriages and families in Jesus name. Amen! I seal up this prayer in the name of the Father, the Son and the Holy Spirit. Amen!

# CHAPTER NINE:
## SECURING GOD'S PRESENCE, GLORY AND HIS BLESSINGS BY THE POWER IN THE BLOOD.

Right from the Old Testament, we see that whenever blood was offered as sacrifice to God, instantly the presence and the glory of God appeared. Once this happened people began to pray and asking for what they desired. What happened here was that the power in the blood gave them access to God's presence.

*Leviticus 9:6-7:*
*And Moses said, "This is what the LORD has commanded you to do so that the glory of the LORD may appear to you."Then Moses said to Aaron, "Come to the altar and sacrifice your sin offering and your burnt offering to purify yourself and the people. Then present the offerings of the people to purify them, making them right with the LORD, just as he has commanded."*

*Leviticus 9:23-24*
*Then Moses and Aaron went into the Tabernacle, and when they came back out, they blessed the people again, and the glory of the LORD appeared to the whole community. Fire blazed forth from the LORD's presence and consumed the burnt offering and the fat on the altar. When the people saw this, they shouted with joy and fell face down on the ground.*

The above scripture is one of the amazing and profound words of God. It reveals the power of the blood in securing God's presence and His glory.

*"...this is what the LORD has commanded you to do so that the glory of the LORD may appear to you."*

What has God commanded? God commanded Aaron to bring the blood of calf and goats as sacrificial offerings on behalf of himself and the entire children of Israel. As Aaron did according to God's command, we see that in verses 22-24, the Bible records what the power in the blood did before the glory of God was revealed among the people:

1) The blood cleansed and atoned for the High Priest, the priests and the people(vs 6)

2) The blood made the people right (or righteous) to make their worship acceptable before God(vs 7)

3) The people were blessed vs 22 and 23

4) The glory of God appeared to the people

   *"...and the glory of the LORD appeared to the whole community."*

5) The presence of God manifested and people saw it. "Fire blazed forth from the LORD's presence..." vs24

6) The joy of the LORD filled the hearts of the people "...they shouted with joy and fell face down on the ground: (vs 24b)

## PRAYER POINTS

Heavenly Father, in the name of Jesus and by the power in the Holy Blood I invoke the authority of your covenant blessings as written in Deuteronomy 28. These blessings have been secured for me and my family when Jesus shed His blood on the cross of Calvary. Therefore, I pronounce these blessings and I call them forth into full operation now.

Therefore, I pray and I confess that:

- My life is abundantly blessed by the blood of Jesus.

- Myself, my wife and my children are blessed by the blood of Jesus.

- My residence, my home and my marriage are blessed by the blood of Jesus.

- I am blessed in the city, in the county and in the borough where I live by the blood of Jesus.

- In Jesus name, my career, my business and my educational undertakings are blessed by the blood of Jesus.

- In Jesus name, wherever I go, and whatever I do shall be blessed by the blood of Jesus.

- I decree that the blood of Jesus will pursue and scatter all my enemies, as they attack in one direction, they will be scattered and fall before me until they all perish in Jesus name.

- In the name of Jesus, the blessing of God is guaranteed on everything that I do. My store houses, my bank account are filled with gold, silver and money in different currencies.

- The blood of Jesus has established me and my family in this land as His holy people.

- By the blood of Jesus, all nations of the world will see me and my household as peculiar people marked, purchased and blessed by the blood of Jesus.

- In the name of Jesus, the LORD gives me prosperity in this nation where I reside with all my family members.

- In Jesus name and by the power in the blood of Jesus, I shall never lack, but I will live in abundance financially, spiritually, materially and in good health.

- **In the name of Jesus all the work that I do either in ministry, business and in other endeavours shall prosper and be blessed abundantly in this nation and other nations where I have influence by the blood of Jesus.**

- **By the blood of Jesus, I am enveloped and protected daily by the presence of God in Jesus name.**

- **In Jesus name I declare and confess that the joy of the LORD shall continually be my strength.**

- **By the blood of Jesus, my family and I are surrounded by the glory of God daily. In Jesus name the people of the world will know that we are chosen in Christ to show forth the glory of God, and when they see us they will stand in awe of us. Amen!**

## CHAPTER TEN:
## UNCOMMON FINANCIAL ABUNDANCE THROUGH THE GRACE IN THE POWER OF HIS BLOOD

*"For ye know the grace of our Lord Jesus Christ, that, though he was rich, yet for your sakes he became poor, that ye through his poverty might be rich."*
*2Corinthians 8:9*

*"Every man according as he purposeth in his heart, so let him give; not grudgingly, or of necessity: for God loveth a cheerful giver. And God is able to make all grace abound toward you; that ye, always having all sufficiency in all things, may abound to every good work:(As it is written, He hath dispersed abroad; he hath given to the poor: his righteousness remaineth for ever. Now he that ministereth seed to the sower both minister bread for your food, and multiply your seed sown, and increase the fruits of your righteousness;)Being enriched in everything to all bountifulness, which causeth through us thanksgiving to God."2Corinthians 9:7-11.*

### PRAYER POINTS:

My Father, in the name of Jesus, I thank You for the grace of financial prosperity made available when Jesus shed His blood on the cross of Calvary. According to YourWordin (2 Corinthians 8:9), I identify fully with the grace of our Lord Jesus Christ made available to me in the form of His kindness, His gracious generosity, His undeserved favour and spiritual blessings. Therefore, I believe that Jesus became poor for my sake that I might become rich and wealthy financially and materially. Jesus bore the curse of poverty for me on the cross of Calvary that I might become partaker of the blessings of Abraham.

For this reason, I confess and I decree that in the name of Jesus and by the power in His blood, and in agreement with the covenant promise of God that: God is able to make all grace (every favour and earthly blessing) come to me in abundance, so that I may always and under all circumstances and whatever the need, be self-sufficient, possessing enough to require no aid or support. In the name of Jesus and by the power in His blood I am furnished, endowed and favoured with abundant financial, material and spiritual blessings for every good work and charitable donation in Jesus name Amen!

In the name of Jesus according to God's promise in Deuteronomy 8:18 I receive creative ability to create wealth, to establish my own business enterprise for the purpose of funding the expansion of the Gospel of the kingdom of God. Also through the blood of Jesus I receive manifold wisdom for witty inventions and innovations of global impact to the praise and the glory of His name.

Father, in the name of Jesus and by the power in His blood, I receive the wisdom of Joseph for real estate and asset management of mega companies, consultant to institutions and to head of nations. By the power in the blood of Jesus, I receive the manifold wisdom of God and the multiple of His grace to become a reformer and problem solver for my generation in Jesus. Amen!

# CHAPTER ELEVEN:
## PROSPERITY OVER WHAT I LAY MY HAND UPON TO DO

The sin of Adam and Eve in the garden of Eden provoked the wrath of God. And for this reason, God judged them by cursing the ground and whatever Adam laid his hands on. From then onwards the descendants of Adam (human race) were subjected to poverty and hard labour, and sorrow. The passage below shows how God cursed the land for the sake of the sin of disobedience of Adam and Eve.

*And unto Adam he said, Because thou hast hearkened unto the voice of thy wife, and hast eaten of the tree, of which I commanded thee, saying, Thou shalt not eat of it: cursed is the ground for thy sake; in sorrow shalt thou eat of it all the days of thy life; Thorns also and thistles shall it bring forth to thee; and thou shalt eat the herb of the field; In the sweat of thy face shalt thou eat bread, till thou return unto the ground; for out of it wast thou taken: for dust thou art, and unto dust shalt thou return.(Genesis 3:17-19)*

But before Jesus was crucified they put upon His head a 'crown of thorns' pressed down on His head with blood streaming over His face. After this, He was then crucified on the cross, with His hands pierced and the blood came out to remove the curse of hard labour with sweat on the face of humanity. Also, the curse of sorrows and economic failure was atoned for. The passage below thus showed the price paid on the cross to remove the curse of economic hardship and sorrow:

### John 19:1-3:
*"Then Pilate therefore took Jesus, and scourged him. And the soldiers platted a crown of thorns, and put it on his head, and they put on him a purple robe, and said, Hail, King of the Jews! and they smote him with their hands."*

### Psalm 1:1-3AMP:
*Blessed [fortunate, prosperous, and favoured by God] is the man who does not walk in the counsel of the wicked [following their advice and example],Nor stand in the path of sinners, Nor sit [down to rest] in the seat of scoffers (ridiculers).But his delight is in the law of the LORD, And on His law [His precepts and teachings] he [habitually] meditates day and night. And he will be like a tree firmly planted [and fed] by streams of water, Which yields its fruit in its season; Its leaf does not wither; And in whatever he does, he prospers [and comes to maturity].*

### Deuteronomy 28:8
*The LORD will command the blessings upon me in my storehouses and in all that I undertake, and He will bless me in the land which the LORD my God gives me.*

## PRAYER POINTS

1) In the name of Jesus and by the power in His blood I confess that whatsoever I lay my hand upon shall prosper. The Word of God have promised me that He will command the blessings upon my life, my storehouses and upon all my undertakings. By the power in the blood of Jesus I declare upon heaven to give rain of prosperity over my life at the right season. In Jesus name all the works of my hands are blessed and established by the prevailing power in His blood. Amen!

2) In the name of Jesus, I disannul all satanic handwritings and accusations directed against my destiny, my progress and all areas of my influence. I invoke the authority of the Word of God and what the blood of Jesus did on the cross of Calvary as testified in God's Word

3) In Jesus name, I pray that I will walk continually in the reality of the accomplished work of redemption on the cross of Calvary.Amen!

# CHAPTER TWELVE:
## MY LIFE IS PURCHASED, PROTECTED AND PRESERVED BY THE BLOOD OF JESUS.

*Acts 20:28:*
*"Take heed therefore unto yourselves and to all the flock, over which the Holy Ghost hath made you overseers, to feed the church of God which He hath purchased with His own blood."*

*1 Corinthians 7:23:*
*"Ye are bought with a price; be ye not the servants of men."*

*1 Corinthians 6:20:*
*"For ye are bought with a price. Therefore, glorify God in your body and in your spirit, which are God's."*

*1 Peter 1:18-19:*
*"Forasmuch as ye know that ye were not redeemed with corruptible things, as silver and gold, from your vain conversation received by tradition from your fathers; But with the precious blood of Christ, as of a lamb without blemish and without spot:"*

## PRAYER POINTS:

1) Father of life, I thank You for Your mercy and abundant love with which You love me. Your love towards me is expressed when Jesus, Your only begotten son shed His blood and died for me on the cross of Calvary. Also, He rose up on the third day for my justification.

   Therefore, in the name of Jesus I affirm and confess that my life, the life of my family members are purchased, protected and preserved from satanic attack in different manifestations.

2) In the name of Jesus, I forbid the evil hand of the enemies to touch me or any member of my family. The Word of God says (Psalm 125:3), the rod of the wicked shall not rest upon the lot of the righteous. Therefore, I and every member of my family are marked by the power in the blood of Jesus.

   Every evil word, incantations, witchcraft prayers, enchantment from human tongue against me or any members of my family shall not proper.

3) By the blood of Jesus, I disannul and neutralise, satanic libations, evil spells, curses, and cultic prayers directed towards my destiny, my success, my

progress, my health and my breakthrough. It shall not rest on me or upon any member of my family. I decree and declare that in Jesus name it shall be returned back to the senders wherever they are, in Jesus name. Amen!

## CHAPTER THIRTEEN:
## CANOPY OF DIVINE SECURITY.
### PSALM 91:1-16

**PRAYERS:**

I, (put your name) that dwell under the secret place of the Most High shall abide under the shadow of the almighty.

I will say of the LORD, He is my refuge and my fortress: my God; in Him I trust, surely He shall deliver me from the snare of the fowler, and from the noisome pestilence. He shall cover me with His feathers, and under His wings shall I trust: His truth shall be my shield and buckler. I shall not be afraid for the terror by night; nor for the arrow that flieth by day; Nor for the pestilence that walketh in the darkness; nor for the destruction that wasteth at noon day.

A thousand shall fall by my side and ten thousand at my right hand; but it shall not come near me. Only with my eyes shall I behold and see the reward of the wicked.

Because I have made the LORD which is my refuge, even the Most High, my habitation;

There shall no evil befall me, neither shall any plague come near my dwelling. For He shall give His angels charge over me to keep me in all my ways, the angels of the LORD shall bear me up in their hands, so that I will not dash my foot against a stone.

I shall tread upon the lion and adder: the young lion and the dragon I shall trample under my feet. Because I have set my love upon God, therefore the LORD will deliver me: The LORD will set me on high, because I know His name.

I shall call upon the LORD and He will answer me: The LORD will be with me in trouble; the LORD will deliver me and honour me.

The LORD will satisfy me with long life and He will show me His salvation. Amen! I confess this prayer over my life and over the members of my family; in the name of the Father, the Son and the Holy Spirit, in Jesus name. Amen!

## CHAPTER FOURTEEN:
## ENFORCING THE POWER IN THE BLOOD OF JESUS AGAINST THE ADVERSARY

### PRAYERS:

1) By the power in the blood of Jesus, I enforce and I put a stop with immediate effect to the source of all the problems in my life, family, children, business in Jesus name. In Jesus name I put a stop to the evil intentions of the wicked and the adversary.

*Psalm 7:9-11:*
*Oh let the wickedness of the wicked come to an end; but establish the just: for the righteous God trieth the hearts and reins. My defence is of God, which saveth the upright in heart. God judgeth the righteous, and God is angry with the wicked every day.*

2) By the power in the blood of Jesus, I decree freedom and total deliverance from the influences of demonic forces that have been working against my progress, success, prosperity and breakthrough in my relationship, family and in every aspect of my life in Jesus name. Amen!

*"If it had not been the LORD who was on our side, now may Israel say; If it had not been the LORD who was on our side, when men rose up against us: Then they had swallowed us up quick, when their wrath was kindled*

*against us: Then the waters had overwhelmed us, the stream had gone over our soul: Then the proud waters had gone over our soul. Blessed be the LORD, who hath not given us as a prey to their teeth. Our soul is escaped as a bird out of the snare of the fowlers: the snare is broken, and we are escaped. Our help is in the name of the LORD, who made heaven and earth."*
*(Psalm 124:1-8).*

3) According to the Word of God and by the prevailing power of the blood of Jesus I am released and set free from every demonic chains, fetters, snares of the enemies, satanic embargoes, bondages of any kind, limitations and anti- progressive spirit

4) In Jesus name I have escaped from the snare of the fowlers and satanic decoy set for me by satanic human agents who appear as friends. I am standing by faith in Christ while I see my enemies falling before me. I am victorious in Jesus name. Amen!

5) By the power in the blood of Jesus, I am totally set free from the effect of manmade law, decrees, policies, edicts, etc which Satan has set up to work against my progress, business, breakthrough, my family, etc. In the name of Jesus, I am delivered.

*"And you who were dead in trespasses and in the uncircumcision of your flesh (your sensuality, your sinful carnal nature), [God] brought to life together with [Christ], having [freely] forgiven us all our transgressions, having cancelled and blotted out and wiped away the handwriting of the note (bond) with its legal decrees and demands which was in force and stood against us (hostile to us). This [note with its regulations, decrees, and demands] He set aside and cleared completely out of our way by nailing it to [His] cross.[God] disarmed the principalities and powers that were ranged against us and made a bold display and public example of them, in triumphing over them in Himandin it [the cross]."*
*Colossians 2:13-15 AMPC*

**By the power in the blood of Jesus, I command total restoration of all the blessings, opportunities, privileges and entitlements that I have been denied in the past years. I command restoration now, in Jesus Mighty name according to Joel 2:21-27:**

*"Fear not, O land; be glad and rejoice: for the LORD will do great things. Be not afraid, ye beasts of the field: for the pastures of the wilderness do spring, for the tree beareth her fruit, the fig tree and the vine do yield their strength. Be glad then, ye children of Zion, and rejoice in the LORD your God: for he hath given you the former rain moderately, and he will cause to come down for you the rain, the former rain, and the latter rain in the first month. And the floors shall be full of wheat, and the vats shall overflow with wine and oil. And I will restore to you the years that the locust hath eaten, the cankerworm, and the caterpiller, and the*

*palmerworm, my great army which I sent among you.*
*And ye shall eat in plenty, and be satisfied, and praise*
*the name of the LORD your God, that hath dealt*
*wondrously with you: and my people shall never be*
*ashamed. And ye shall know that I am in the midst of*
*Israel, and that I am the LORD your God, and none else:*
*and my people shall never be ashamed."*

6) **In Jesus name I turn the battle against all my adversaries, and I command them to turn back and back out of my life and out of my territories in Jesus name. I put my faith in the power that is in the blood of Jesus and therefore I decree and declare that every battle and arrow set up against me, my family, my ministry, my business undertakings or my destiny return to the senders by the blood of Jesus.**

**And because my faith is in the blood of Jesus the only begotten Son of the living God, I command victory over all my adversaries who tend to oppose my progress and my destiny.**

**In Jesus name and by the power in His blood I and every member of my family will live long to fulfil our destiny and enjoy the abundant life**

**in Christ to the fullest in Jesus name, Amen!**

**I RECEIVE ANSWERS TO ALL MY PRAYERS IN JESUS NAME. AMEN!**

# CHAPTER FIFTEEN:
## THE POWER AND THE BENEFITS OF SPRINKLING THE BLOOD OF JESUS BY FAITH

*So shall He startle and sprinkle many nations...*
*(Isaiah 52:15)*

*And to Jesus the Mediator of the new covenant, and to the blood of sprinkling, that speaketh better things than that of Abel.(Hebrews 12:24)*

There is a need to learn from the children of Israel about what God taught them on 'how to use the power of 'blood sprinkling' to defeat the purpose and the intentions of Pharaoh. This secret was revealed to them through the prophetic ministry of Prophet Moses.

The children of Israel were ransomed and delivered from the power of Pharaoh and the Egyptian bondage by making use of the secret and the power of blood sprinkling. The power of blood sprinkling defeated Pharaoh and liberated them from his oppressive rule.

The Lord gave me the revelation about the secret and the power of sprinkling the blood of Jesus by faith as a secret weapon against Satanic attack and an antidote for securing uncommon favour. We are going to use the revelation of blood sprinkling in relation and in parallel with how the children of Israel made use of it in Egypt. The power in the shed blood is not effective until the action of sprinkling takes place.

This is the revelation which the Lord want me to pass to the Body of Christ, since Jesus has already made His blood (shed blood) available to us. Therefore, what we need to do is to use our faith as 'hyssop' to do the sprinkling daily.

In this chapter I will like to point our attention to some points about the application of blood sprinkling with related prayer.

## BLOOD SPRINKLING RELEASES PLAGUE OF JUDGEMENT OVER YOUR ENEMIES.

As we sprinkle the blood of Jesus by faith, we are releasing plagues of judgement thereby inflicting pain over our enemies. This is exactly what God asked the children of Israel to do.

*Exodus 11:1*
*Then the Lord said to Moses, Yet will I bring one plague*
*more on Pharaoh and on Egypt; afterwards he will let*
*you go. When he lets you go from here, he will thrust*
*you out altogether.*

*Exodus 12:21-23,29*
*"Then Moses called for all the elders of Israel, and said*
*to them, Go forth, select and take a lamb according to*
*your families and kill the Passover [lamb].And you*
*shall take a bunch of hyssop, dip it in the blood in the*
*basin, and touch the lintel above the door and the two*
*side posts with the blood; and none of you shall go out*
*of his house until morning. For the Lord will pass*
*through to slay the Egyptians; and when He sees the*
*blood upon the lintel and the two side posts, the Lord*
*will pass over the door and will not allow the destroyer*
*to come into your houses to slay you... At midnight the*
*Lord slew every firstborn in the land of Egypt, from the*
*firstborn of Pharaoh who sat on his throne to the*
*firstborn of the prisoner in the dungeon, and all the*
*firstborn of the livestock."*

## PRAYER:

My Father, in the name of Jesus I sprinkle the
blood of Jesus by faith to release plagues of
judgement over my enemies. Wherever they
are, cover my enemies with the garment of
sorrow and pain. As they don't wish me well, I
decree by the power in the blood let
happiness and joy be far away from them. By
faith I sprinkle the blood of Jesus as canopy
of protection over me and over all that
pertain to me in Jesus name. Amen!

**By the power in the blood of Jesus, I pray and I make a demand for the soul of my loved ones who are yet to come to the knowledge of Christ. By faith I sprinkle the blood of Jesus over their lives for the salvation and redemption of their souls wherever they are. Jesus has already been lifted up on the cross and their ransom had been paid for in Jesus name, Amen! Let the blood speak into their spirits and bring them into repentance, giving their lives to Jesus fully. Amen!**

## BLOOD SPRINKLING PROTECT YOU FROM DEMONIC SPELLS

Believers are encouraged to sprinkle the blood of Jesus over their lives daily by faith as a canopy of protection against demonic spells. The reason is that we are constantly living in a wicked or evil infested and ungodly environment. We are living in the perilous time that the Bible talks about which is being govern by satanic system and evil ideology set up to contend against believers and the church of Jesus at large. The Egyptian system forced the children of Israel (the people of God) to worship many strange gods instead of the true God...the God of Abraham, Isaac and Jacob. But God instructed the children of Israel to use hyssop and sprinkle the blood of the prophetic lamb upon their household in other to judge the system and the gods of Egypt.

Remember that as you sprinkle the blood of Jesus over your lives, you are doing it knowing that you are the temple or the house of God.

*Exodus 12:12-13 AMPC*
*For I will pass through the land of Egypt this night and will smite all the firstborn in the land of Egypt, both man and beast; and against all the gods of Egypt I will execute judgment [proving their helplessness]. I am the Lord. The blood shall be for a token or sign to you upon [the door posts of] the houses where you are, [that] when I see the blood, I will pass over you, and no plague shall be upon you to destroy you when I smite the land of Egypt.*

*John 12:31 AMPC*
*"Now the judgment (crisis) of this world is coming on [sentence is now being passed on this world]. Now the ruler (evil genius, prince) of this world shall be cast out (expelled)."*

## PRAYER:

In the name of Jesus, by faith I sprinkle the blood of Jesus upon my life and the live of all members of my family. By the sprinkling of the blood of Jesus Christ we are protected against the influence of satanic systems, evil ideologies and wicked policies established by human agents to contend against my spiritual life, my progress, my ministry, business undertakings or my destiny in general. The Word of God says, no weapon formed against

**me shall prosper, and every tongue that rises against me in judgement is condemned in Jesus name. I pray this same prayer for every member of my family...(husband, wife and children, my siblings, my mother, father, etc). In Jesus name I execute judgement against the adversaries of my progress, success and breakthrough by the blood of Jesus, Amen!**

## BLOOD SPRINKLING SECURES FREEDOM AND UNCOMMON FAVOUR BEFORE YOUR ENEMIES

*Exodus 12:22*
*And ye shall take a bunch of hyssop, and dip it in the blood that is in the basin, and strike the lintel and the two side posts with the blood that is in the basin; and none of you shall go out from the door of his house until the morning.*

*Exodus 12:35-36*
*And the children of Israel did according to the word of Moses, and they borrowed from the Egyptians jewels of silver and jewels of gold and raiment. And the LORD gave the people favor in the sight of the Egyptians, so that they lent unto them such things as they required. And they despoiled the Egyptians.*

We see in the above passage how the sprinkling of the blood activated uncommon favour for wealth transfer from the hand of the Egyptians to the hand of the children of God. The blood gave them advantage over their enemies. This is a lesson we need to learn as believers, learning to sprinkle the blood of Jesus upon ourselves daily by faith as we go out to different places (workplace, journey, going for an interview, Court cases, etc).

### PRAYER:

**In the name of Jesus, and by the power in the Holy Blood of Jesus, I sprinkle the blood of Jesus by faith upon my life and members of my family, for uncommon favour and uncommon advantage over the enemies of my life. I also pray and legislate by the power in the blood of Jesus that I will always be surrounded by the atmosphere and an aura of uncommon favour and unusual advantage in every sphere of my influence. I pray this prayer in the name of the Father, the Son and the Holy Spirit. Amen!**

## THE SPRINKLING OF THE BLOOD PERMITS GOD TO JUDGE OTHER gods IN EGYPT.

Believers are encouraged to command each day, early in the morning by sprinkling the blood of Jesus over the atmosphere of their boroughs and the nation where they live.

*"Have you ever commanded the morning at any time during your life? (Job 38:12 ISV)*

83

It is vital to secure divine protection daily by invoking the power in the blood of Jesus as we go out to different places. This is because each day is full of evil as Jesus revealed in His message on the sermon on the mountain.

*But seek ye first the kingdom of God, and His righteousness, and all these things shall be added unto you. Take therefore no thought for the things of itself, sufficient unto the day is the evil thereof.*
*(Matthew 6:33-34)*

*AS YOU WAKE UP EARLY IN THE MORNING AND SPRINKLE THE BLOOD OF JESUS OVER THE ATMOSPHERE, WHAT HAPPENS IS THAT YOU ARE UPSETTING EVIL PLANS OF SATAN FOR THAT DAY IN VARIETY OF WAYS.*

**EXODUS 12:12-13**
*For I will pass through the land of Egypt this night, and will smite all the firstborn in the land of Egypt, both man and beast; and against all the gods of Egypt I will execute judgment: I am the LORD. And the blood shall be to you for a token upon the houses where ye are: and when I see the blood, I will pass over you, and the plague shall not be upon you to destroy you, when I smite the land of Egypt.*

Furthermore, as we sprinkle the blood of Jesus into the atmosphere early in the morning, we cleanse and purify our community of sinful activities. We also execute judgement and inhibit

the activities of unclean spirits, the negative
activities of the false prophets and idolatry

*"In that day there shall be a fountain opened to the
house of David and to the inhabitants of Jerusalem for
sin and for uncleanness. And it shall come to pass in
that day, saith the LORD of hosts, that I will cut off the
names of the idols out of the land, and they shall no
more be remembered: and also I will cause the
prophets and the unclean spirit to pass out of the
land."(Zechariah 13:1-2).*

## PRAYERS:

Almighty God and Father of life, I pray in the
name of Jesus that by the power in the blood
of Jesus Iam delivered from all evil
occurrences assigned by Satan to cause havoc
on daily basis in the lives of people. I decree
in Jesus name that this day from dawn to
dusk will work in my favour. I sprinkle the
blood of Jesus over myself and every member
of my family. We activate our angels to
preserve and protect us against dangers and
evil occurrences in the air, on the road and
over the sea, in Jesus name. Today,by the
blood of Jesus I upset the evil intensions and
plans of Satan and his cohorts.

I confess that surely, goodness and mercy
shall follow me all the days of my life: and I

**will dwell in the house of the Lord forever and ever. Amen!**

# THE POWER IN THE BLOOD OF JESUS HAS THE CAPACITY TO ERASE SATANIC HANDWRITING

*"And you, being dead in your sins and the uncircumcision of your flesh, hath he quickened together with him, having forgiven you all trespasses; blotting out the handwriting of ordinances that was against us, which was contrary to us, and took it out of the way, nailing it to his cross; and having spoiled principalities and powers, he made a shew of them openly, triumphing over them in it."*
*(Colossians 2:13-15)*

### PRAYER:

My Father in heaven, I put my faith in the power that is in the Holy Blood of Jesus. Therefore, in Jesus name I decree and declare that by the power in the blood of Jesus, I erase the handwriting of Satan against my destiny and the destiny of any member of my family. By the power in the blood of Jesus I delete poverty, bareness, broken marriage, premature death, ungodly generational history, curses, unprofitable business, every form of restriction and limitation in Jesus name.

**By the blood of Jesus, a new history is written for me, old history that was against me has been blotted out in Jesus name.**

**By the atoning power of the blood of Jesus, I am a new creation, old things and old history are passed away and I walk in the newness of life in Jesus name. Jesus, the Lamb of God has shed His blood to redeem and re-write my history.**

*Exodus 12: 1-3:*
*And the LORD spake unto Moses and Aaron in the land of Egypt, saying, This month shall be unto you the beginning of months: it shall be the first month of the year to you. Speak ye unto all the congregation of Israel, saying, In the tenth day of this month they shall take to them every man a lamb, according to the house of their fathers, a lamb for an house:*

**By the power in the blood of Jesus I confess my new testimony and who I am according to 2Corinthians 5:17:**

*"Therefore if any man be in Christ, he is a new creature: old things are passed away; behold, all things are become new."*

**I thank God for being a new creation...Hallelujah!!**

**LET THE BLOOD SPEAK!**

# ABOUT THE AUTHOR

Johnson Akinfenwa is the President of Joshua Generation World Outreach Ministries and Overseer of Joshua Generation Christ Tabernacle (the church arm of JGWOM). Having been in Pastoral Ministry for nearly three decades, he was ordained and consecrated to the office of a Prophet in 2007, officiated by Dr Hugh Osgood, President of Free Churches in England and Wales and also the Presiding Apostle of Churches in Community International (CiC).

Prophet Johnson is passionate to see the restoration and effective function of true prophetic office these days as a channel by which God speaks to the church and the world at large.

He ministers the word of God with sharp prophetic insight. He is a prophetic teacher and itinerant conference speaker. Churches, Ministries, Nations and individual have benefitted from his Prophetic Ministry. As the Director of Voice of Prophecy International Outreach (VOPIO), he featured on TV, sharing God's mind prophetically to the church and the nations. As a praying prophet, he is a convenor of an Annual National Fasting and Prayer of Repentance, Revival and Healing for the United Kingdom. He is also the co-ordinator of National Prophetic Prayer Movement, a movement for Spiritual Awakening and Revival of Christian heritage in different regions of the UK.

He is the author of many books including: Praying Prophet and Prophetic Intercessors, The King, The Bride and the Spirit, Unveiling Resurrection Power, How to use the power in the blood of Jesus for a result-oriented prayer, We are sons of God with power.

Johnson holds a Bachelor degree in pure chemistry and counts it as a great honour to be called into the service of the Kingdom as a Prophet to the nations. He is married to his lovely wife, Pastor Funmilola Akinfenwa and they are blessed with five children.

All glory and honour be ascribed unto God. Amen!

## PERSONAL ENDORSEMENT

God has made the blood of Jesus available to us as our weapon of warfare. What we need to do is to deep our faith in the prevailing power of the blood. God speaks mercy, victory, blessings, breakthrough, success, redemption, justification, cleansing, peace and so on to the Body of Christ through the blood of Jesus today.

Obviously, God has made the holy Blood of the LORD Jesus Christ available to us as our weapon of warfare. What we really need to do is to maintain our deep faith in the prevailing power of the blood in making our prayer effective and result-oriented.

*"And to Jesus, the Mediator of a new covenant [uniting God and man], and to the sprinkled blood, which speaks [of mercy], a better and nobler and more gracious message than the blood of Abel [which cried out for vengeance]."(Hebrews 12: 24 AMPC).*

Information about the author, other books by the same author, CD/DVD, prophecies, events, invitations to conferences etc:

Email: voicepio@yahoo.co.uk

Website: www.vopio.org.


Prophet Johnson Akinfenwa.
Director,
Voice of Prophecy International Outreach.
(Hebrews 12:24)